Reach Higher

Reach Higher

An Inspiring Photo Celebration of First Lady Michelle Obama

AMANDA LUCIDON

Former Official White House Photographer

Adapted from the *New York Times* Bestseller *Chasing Light*

Crown Books for Young Readers ♔ New York

For Alan, Eden & Kai

All rights reserved. Published in the United States by Crown Books for Young Readers, an imprint of Random House Children's Books, a division of Penguin Random House LLC, New York.
This work is based on *Chasing Light: Michelle Obama Through the Lens of a White House Photographer*, copyright © 2017 by Amanda Lucidon. Published in hardcover in the United States by Ten Speed Press, an imprint of the Crown Publishing Group, a division of Penguin Random House LLC, New York, in 2017.

Crown and the colophon are registered trademarks of Penguin Random House LLC.
All photographs are by Amanda Lucidon, with the exception of those appearing on page 15, by Chuck Kennedy, and page 17, by Lawrence Jackson.

Visit us on the Web! rhcbooks.com

Educators and librarians, for a variety of teaching tools, visit us at RHTeachersLibrarians.com

Library of Congress Cataloging-in-Publication Data is available upon request.
ISBN 978-0-525-64400-2 (trade)—ISBN 978-0-525-64402-6 (lib. bdg.)—ISBN 978-0-525-64401-9 (ebook)
MANUFACTURED IN CHINA
10 9 8 7 6 5 4 3 2 1
First Edition

Contents

CHAPTER 1
What Does the First Lady Do?   11

CHAPTER 2
What Does a White House Photographer Do?   14

CHAPTER 3
The People's House   19

CHAPTER 4
Welcoming the World   33

CHAPTER 5
Role Model   51

CHAPTER 6
Reaching Higher   67

CHAPTER 7
Art Lover   75

CHAPTER 8
Visitor-in-Chief   85

Leaving the White House   106

Acknowledgments   108

What Does the First Lady Do?

A First Lady is not elected. She immediately gets the job when her spouse is inaugurated as President of the United States. The Constitution doesn't define the responsibilities of the job, so it's up to each First Lady to make the role her own. Although the First Lady doesn't get paid for her efforts, her work is extremely important to the country. The causes she champions, her interactions with the public, and her hosting of world leaders and their spouses help to shape each First Lady's legacy. Michelle Obama put her unique stamp on the role through her hard work, dedication, keen intelligence, commitment to family, and sense of humor. She led by example and became a role model and inspiration to our nation.

Martha Washington was the first "first spouse." But Dolley Madison was the first presidential spouse to be referred to as First Lady. She had many years of practice in the role, first for eight years as a stand-in hostess for the widowed Thomas Jefferson, then for the two terms of her own husband, James Madison. Dolley was renowned for bringing people from various backgrounds and beliefs together, in addition to rescuing a famous portrait of George Washington when the White House was burned by the British during the War of 1812.

President and Mrs. Obama smile at each other as they walk from Marine One on the South Lawn of the White House. September 29, 2015

President and Mrs. Obama share a special moment in the Diplomatic Reception Room of the White House. This image has become one of the most widely shared photos of the First Couple. March 27, 2015

CHAPTER 2

What Does a White House Photographer Do?

In January 2009, I was inspired to photograph Barack Obama's first inauguration as a member of the crowd. A few years later, I was surprised by a phone call from the Chief White House Photographer, Pete Souza, who invited me to become an official White House photographer covering President Obama and First Lady Michelle Obama. I felt so honored to have the opportunity to document the important personal and public moments of our first African American First Family!

John F. Kennedy was the first president to have a White House photographer. Since then, every president except Jimmy Carter has chosen a photographer to share important moments of the presidency.

Meeting Mrs. Obama for the first time was a blur. I was so excited and nervous. And as I watched other people meet her, some of them laughed, some cried, and some just covered their mouths in awe. Mrs. Obama met so many people all the time, but they were not used to meeting her. Witnessing these interactions made me realize that if I was going to do my job effectively, I'd have to find a way to get comfortable in Mrs. Obama's presence.

This was the first time I met Mrs. Obama, in the Lower Cross Hall of the White House. It's not often that I find myself on the other side of the camera. I was so grateful that my fellow White House photographer Chuck Kennedy took a photo of this special moment. June 5, 2013

There was no routine day for a White House photographer. I covered meetings, speeches, performances, tapings, state visits, and travel, in the United States and abroad. It could be busy and exciting or slow and routine—but slow days could become busy at any minute. Even though I spent most of my time photographing Mrs. Obama, I also covered events with the President.

A certain phrase always stayed with me: "The motorcade only waits for one person . . . and it's not you." Missing the motorcade or plane was my biggest fear. It could mean there would be no official photographs of an event. So I always made sure to be early.

Being a White House photographer allowed me to witness history in the making. I learned so much from the President and First Lady. I found inspiration in their leadership and humanity. It was an experience that changed my life.

My fellow White House photographer
Lawrence Jackson photographed
me waiting with the press pool for
the arrival of President Xi Jinping
of China and Madame Peng Liyuan
during the State Arrival Ceremony.
September 25, 2015

CHAPTER 3

The People's House

A longtime usher called the White House a "living, breathing museum." That's a perfect way to describe it, because it captures the history of the building and its furnishings and the people who came before us.

John Adams and his wife, Abigail, were the first presidential family to live in the newly built President's Palace, as it was called at the time. James Madison and his wife, Dolley, were the last, because the British burned down the building in 1814 during the War of 1812. Since it was rebuilt in 1817, several presidents have renovated or expanded the White House. It now has 132 rooms, 35 bathrooms, and 6 floors. The first floor of the residence is called the State Floor, where most of the official functions and receptions take place.

Over the years, it was also called the President's House and the Executive Mansion, until President Theodore Roosevelt called it the White House in 1901 and the name was embraced.

President and Mrs. Obama made it their mission to open the doors of the White House to as many people as possible. They wanted everyone to experience the history of the building that the First Lady often called the People's House. Everyone was welcome.

The White House, lit with the colors of the rainbow to celebrate the Supreme Court ruling that legalized same-sex marriage. June 26, 2015

Above: When Mrs. Obama learned that Kulsoom Nawaz Sharif, the wife of Pakistan's prime minister, enjoyed poetry, she arranged a poetry recital in her guest's honor in the Blue Room. October 23, 2013

Right: First Lady Michelle Obama hugs Keniya Brown, a guest invited by DC Child and Family Services foster care system, in the Blue Room before the Take Your Daughters and Sons to Work Day event. April 20, 2016

The Blue Room is the same shape and size as the Oval Office. Through the years, it has been used as the formal room where presidents receive guests, from kings and queens to celebrities and sports figures to teachers and students.

Martin Van Buren gave the room its color scheme in 1837, using paint, furnishings, and fabrics. Then in 1886, Grover Cleveland became the only president to get married at the White House, and he chose the Blue Room for the big event. Mrs. Obama often hosted spouses of foreign leaders and other important guests here.

Next to the Blue Room is the richly colored Red Room. This room has been used for different purposes over the years, from Dolley Madison's frequent receptions, known as her "Wednesday drawing rooms," to small presidential dinner parties. It was also Mary Todd Lincoln's favorite sitting room, where she received her guests. But the Obamas mostly used it as a waiting room for events that took place in the State Dining Room next door.

" *Each of us* has something to *contribute to* the life of *this nation.* "

Mrs. Obama waits in the Red Room as she watches Alicia Keys introduce her to the audience gathered to watch a special movie screening in the State Dining Room.
January 15, 2014

The East Room is the largest space in the White House. Celebratory events in the East Room have included large State Dinners, White House weddings—including those of Alice Roosevelt, Lynda Bird Johnson, and Tricia Nixon—and performances by musicians, dancers, and other artists. More somber moments have taken place in the room as well, including funerals for seven presidents, presidential family members like young Willie Lincoln, and other dignitaries.

Beyond its official functions, some White House children have used it as their big playroom. Tad Lincoln rode across the room on a chair pulled by a pair of goats. Teddy Roosevelt's children liked to roller-skate from one side of the room to the other. And Susan Ford had her school's prom there.

First Lady Michelle Obama and her guests watch a performance of *Finding Neverland* during *Broadway at the White House* in the East Room. November 16, 2015

The State Dining Room is used for large formal gatherings, such as receptions, luncheons, and official State Dinners, when the president entertains visiting heads of state. It was originally Thomas Jefferson's private office, but James Madison turned it into a dining room. The room was enlarged and redecorated by many different presidents. The furniture is often removed to host performances and other events.

When I saw a determined group of young black girls practicing an African-inspired dance in the State Dining Room under Abraham Lincoln's portrait, I knew I was witnessing a special moment in history.

Left: Students rehearse in the State
Dining Room for their performance
in the East Room, during a day-long
dance workshop in celebration of
Black History Month, highlighting
the contributions African American
women have made to dance.
February 8, 2016

Above: The First Lady with students
in the State Dining Room after their
dance workshop performance.
February 8, 2016

27

Mrs. Obama redesigned the Old Family Dining Room to be a showcase of modern art and design and opened it to the public on White House tours for the first time in history.

My favorite art in the room is *Resurrection* (left), a painting by Alma Thomas, the first African American woman to have her art included in the White House permanent collection.

Before Jacqueline Kennedy moved the family dining room to the private residence upstairs, previous First Families had used this room for their meals.

Susan Pocharski from *More* magazine, First Lady Michelle Obama, and actress Meryl Streep share a laugh in the Old Family Dining Room during an interview conducted by the First Lady as part of her role as the first guest editor in the magazine's history.
February 24, 2015

John Adams, the first president to live in the White House, used the Green Room as a guest bed-chamber. When his successor, Thomas Jefferson, restored the room to its original purpose as a dining room, the only green in the room was the green canvas floor cloth. Here, President James Madison signed the declaration of war that started the War of 1812, which eventually led to the burning of the White House.

After the White House was rebuilt, President James Monroe decorated the room with green silks and made it his Card Room. John Quincy Adams later named it the Green Drawing Room. Most modern First Families have used the room for small formal gatherings, like when Eleanor Roosevelt received famed pilot Amelia Earhart here.

The Obamas often used the room to gather before joining larger events taking place on either side of the Green Room, in the East Room or the Blue Room.

Mrs. Obama, Dr. Jill Biden, and staff share a moment in the Green Room before the final Joining Forces event to honor military families at the White House.
November 14, 2016

CHAPTER 4

Welcoming the World

Through the lens of my camera, I watched Mrs. Obama make everyone feel at home. Her guests felt loved because of her kind words and thoughtful consideration. She hosted foreign leaders and their spouses with dignity and grace. She inspired students through arts education by highlighting their talents and cheering on their performances.

I've always admired her ability to ignite a spark in young people, especially those who struggle to see the light inside themselves. She opened the door to so many people who didn't feel they deserved to be in such an important place. And she always reassured them that they were smart, talented, special, and deserving.

" Our country is **counting on all of you** to step forward and **help us** with the *work* that remains. "

Mrs. Obama speaks to the new class of White House interns—college students eager to learn how the government works. As part of their program, they heard from different speakers, including the First Lady. She loved to answer their questions and made them laugh to help them feel more at ease. April 2, 2014

The President and First Lady welcomed Pope Francis to the White House during his first visit to the United States. It was a history-making moment as the first pope from South America was greeted by the first African American President.

Above and right: President Obama, Mrs. Obama, and Pope Francis wave from the Blue Room Balcony to the huge crowd on the South Lawn waiting to greet the new pope. September 23, 2015

Several times a year, the White House hosts a State Arrival Ceremony to welcome foreign dignitaries and strengthen the bonds between countries. These days are filled with formal ceremonies, speeches, and special performances.

Mrs. Obama learned that Mrs. Akie Abe, wife of the prime minister of Japan, loved dogs. So she brought the First Family's dogs, Bo and Sunny, to meet Mrs. Abe after the Japan State Arrival Ceremony. To my surprise, the First Ladies sat on the floor in their formal attire as they laughed and played with the dogs. It was such a sweet and informal moment—I could imagine both women as little girls doing the same thing.

Bo and Sunny greet Mrs. Obama and Mrs. Akie Abe of Japan in the Ground Floor Corridor of the White House. April 28, 2015

The US Army Old Guard Fife and Drum Corps performs during the Singapore State Arrival Ceremony on the South Lawn of the White House. August 2, 2016

State Dinners honor visiting leaders and their guests. These formal events can be held on the South Lawn or in one of the rooms of the White House. The food and entertainment pay tribute to the guests and their country. The First Lady acts as the official hostess—choosing the guest list, the menu, the flowers, and the decorations. The Obamas hosted fourteen State Dinners.

Above: The First Lady's place setting at the State Dinner for the US–Nordic Leaders' Summit. May 13, 2016

Right: The President and First Lady enter the State Dinner. May 13, 2016

The Obamas were determined to welcome as many people as possible to the White House during the holidays. Over their eight holiday seasons, they hosted almost a half million guests and served 200,000 holiday cookies. The first visitors of the season were military families, to honor and celebrate their special contribution to the country.

Above: Mrs. Obama welcomes the military families who have come to view the White House holiday decorations. November 29, 2016

Left: The First Lady, with Obama family pets Bo and Sunny, takes a sneak peek at the official White House Christmas tree, an 18.5-foot Fraser fir, as it arrives by horse-drawn wagon at the North Portico of the White House. November 27, 2015

Mrs. Obama started a tradition of a Kids' State Dinner in 2012, featuring the winning delicious and nutritious recipes from her national Healthy Lunchtime Challenge. The event was patterned after official State Dinners, but instead of honoring foreign leaders, Mrs. Obama celebrated children as Healthy Food Ambassadors from every state, along with their parent or guardian.

Left: Mrs. Obama speaks at the fifth and final Kids' State Dinner. July 14, 2016

Above: Guests line up in the State Dining Room to meet Mrs. Obama before the fourth Kids' State Dinner in the East Room of the White House. July 10, 2015

Above and right: President and Mrs. Obama lead the crowd in a dramatic reading of *Where the Wild Things Are* by Maurice Sendak, one of the President's favorite books, during the Easter Egg Roll. March 28, 2016

The White House Easter Egg Roll has been a beloved annual tradition since President Rutherford B. Hayes started it in 1878. The Obamas welcomed 35,000 people each year to this fun event, and more than 250,000 people between 2009 and 2016. For their final year, the event honored the First Lady's many initiatives. To celebrate Let's Move!, they even added the first White House Fun Run.

Fifty Girl Scouts camped out on the South Lawn for the first-ever White House Campout. During the day, the girls learned how to pitch tents, tie knots, and climb a rock wall. At night, they studied the sky with NASA scientists and astronaut Cady Coleman and sang campfire songs. The evening included a special visit from President Obama, who joked, "What are you doing in my yard?"

The event celebrated the one hundredth anniversary of America's National Parks—including the White House, which is an official National Park.

Left: Mrs. Obama watches with pride as Girl Scouts climb the rock wall during the White House Campout on the South Lawn. June 30, 2015

Above: The President and First Lady sing songs during the White House Campout. June 30, 2015

CHAPTER 5
Role Model

Most modern First Ladies use their special role to shine light on the issues that are important to them. Mrs. Obama used her voice to inspire and empower people throughout the country and the world.

Many of the First Lady's efforts were aimed at helping young people get healthier. She started the White House Kitchen Garden to highlight the importance of eating nutritious food, and she encouraged children to be active and maintain a healthy weight through her Let's Move! initiative.

Other First Ladies who have championed causes related to children include Lou Henry Hoover, who became honorary president of the Girl Scouts; Nancy Reagan, with her Just Say No anti drug campaign; and Laura Bush, who supported reading and literacy.

> *Success* isn't about how much money you make, it's about the *difference* you make in *people's lives.*

Mrs. Obama and graffiti artist Mr. Brainwash look at a mural he painted during an event marking the one-year anniversary of Let Girls Learn, at Union Market in Washington, DC. The many hearts represent the 62 million girls around the world who are not in school. March 8, 2016

Mrs. Obama adores kids and puppies. This taping on the South Lawn seemed to have the perfect ingredients to make a great video promoting the Let's Move! campaign. But little kids and puppies are totally unpredictable.

The film directors had to figure out how to keep the kids' attention while also making sure the puppies didn't run away. Luckily, I was there to capture the scene, not wrangle the puppies.

The First Lady tapes a Let's Move! video to be shown during Animal Planet's *Puppy Bowl*, with students from Harriet Tubman Elementary School, the Obamas' dog Bo, and puppies! October 28, 2013

Mrs. Obama also knew the power of a quiet, more personal moment. Several times a year, she made surprise visits to children's hospitals. She would talk to patients and their families about school, favorite hobbies, and their treatment. She could be a nurturing mother, a sympathetic listener, or a silly friend—whatever was needed at the time.

We brought cookies made by the White House pastry chef to leave with the kids. Their faces would light up when she gave them cookies shaped and frosted to look like Bo and Sunny.

Mrs. Obama visits Camron Stevens in his room at St. Jude Children's Research Hospital in Memphis, Tennessee. September 17, 2014

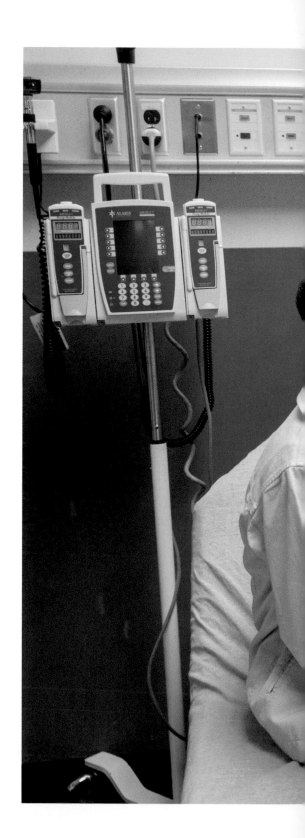

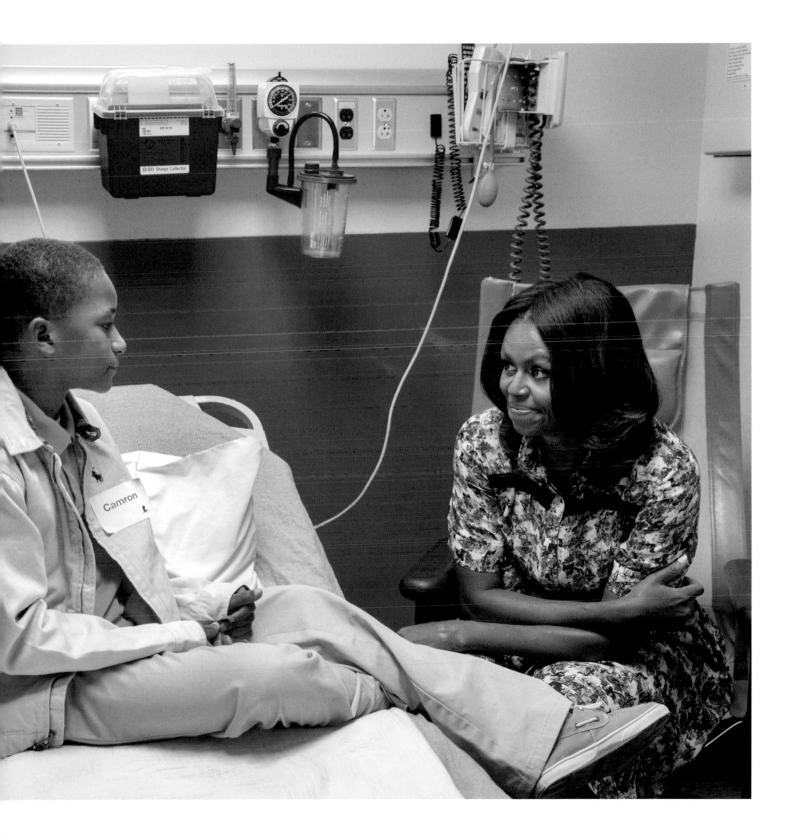

Above: Mrs. Obama demonstrates her boxing skills for a Let's Move! video. May 12, 2015

Right: Mrs. Obama participates in a fencing demonstration as Ibtihaj Muhammad, the first American woman to compete in the Olympics wearing a hijab, looks on during the 2016 Olympics 100 Days Out event in Times Square, New York. April 27, 2016

Mrs. Obama wasn't afraid to be silly, dance, sing, or act in a funny skit to make her point about an important issue. She even harnessed social media and enlisted the star power of celebrities to get the word out about her efforts so she could make a difference in more people's lives.

Left. First Lady Michelle Obama tapes a Funny or Die segment to promote healthy eating with Billy Eichner of *Billy on the Street* and Big Bird at a Safeway in Washington, DC. January 12, 2015

Above: Mrs. Obama teams up with Muppets Rosita and Zari to celebrate the Day of the Girl and to support Let Girls Learn. October 11, 2016

It was a rainy, windy day, and we were glad that the weather cleared long enough for us to visit an urban rooftop garden in New Jersey, one of the stops on Mrs. Obama's school garden tour. She wanted to highlight many of the inspiring and innovative garden programs as part of the Let's Move! initiative.

Students were so excited to show off what they'd learned about composting. They offered Mrs. Obama gardening gloves, but she told the group she didn't mind getting her hands dirty. While demonstrating the different stages of composting, one of the girls found a worm. Mrs. Obama reacted as she lifted the worm up to eye level and everyone laughed. It was a fun moment to document.

Mrs. Obama learns about composting with students at Philip's Academy Charter School in Newark, New Jersey. April 7, 2016

Mrs. Obama first planted her White House Kitchen Garden in 2009. She often invited children to help plant and tend the garden, to show them how food is grown and harvested and to model healthy eating habits.

First Lady Eleanor Roosevelt also planted a garden at the White House, a Victory Garden to encourage families to grow some of their own food to help with shortages during World War II.

Above: Mrs. Obama harvests kale with students in the White House Kitchen Garden. June 6, 2016

Right: Mrs. Obama talks with students during a meal they prepared following the harvest of the White House Kitchen Garden. June 6, 2016

Before the dedication of the White House Kitchen Garden, Mrs. Obama walked under the new arbor with student Tammy Nguyen. Tammy was introducing the First Lady for the garden dedication, as she had introduced her six years earlier during the launch of the First Lady's Let's Move! initiative.

Mrs. Obama stood under the arbor as she spoke:

> "This garden has taught us that if we have the **courage** to plant a seed, then *take care* of it, water it ... [and] *weather the storms* that inevitably come, if we have the courage to do that, we never know what might *grow.*"

The First Lady and Tammy Nguyen walk under the new arbor, which was made from trees found throughout the United States, including pine and walnut harvested from the estates of Thomas Jefferson, James Madison, and James Monroe and the birthplace of Martin Luther King Jr.
October 5, 2015

CHAPTER 6

Reaching Higher

During her eight years as First Lady, Mrs. Obama looked for ways to have a positive impact on people's lives.

Through the Joining Forces initiative, Mrs. Obama worked with Dr. Jill Biden to support veterans and military families. Together they focused on helping returning veterans find new jobs and medical care, and providing services for families that were separated when soldiers were sent overseas for active duty. The First Lady also focused on the importance of education through her Reach Higher and Let Girls Learn initiatives.

" When you've **worked hard** and done well, and walked through that *door of opportunity,* you do not slam it shut behind you. You *reach back,* and you give other folks the same chances that helped you *succeed.* "

Mrs. Obama takes a selfie with a service member following a veterans' job summit at Fort Campbell, Kentucky. April 23, 2014

Above and right: First Lady Michelle Obama and Dr. Jill Biden have fun on the set with Adam Levine and Blake Shelton during rehearsal before the kickoff of the fifth anniversary of their Joining Forces initiative on NBC's *The Voice* in Burbank, California. May 2, 2016

Through Reach Higher, the First Lady challenged young people to continue their education after high school. She talked with students about opportunities and the help that was available to make higher education a reality. She gave several speeches at graduations each year to inspire students nationwide.

This graduation had special meaning for the First Lady. She went to the Dr. Martin Luther King College Preparatory High School graduation on Chicago's South Side—where she grew up—to honor the achievement of the 177 graduates, who had all been accepted to college. She also came to pay tribute to their classmate Hadiya Pendleton, an honors student who was an innocent victim of gang violence just a week after performing at President Obama's second inauguration.

CHAPTER 7

Art Lover

The arts have been a powerful and important part of my life and career. The Obamas recognized the power of the arts to change people's lives and allow them to see new possibilities for the future. For this reason, Mrs. Obama dedicated herself to providing opportunities for children to create their own art and music and supported programs that gave young people the chance to interact with prominent artists and experience live performances.

> " My parents always made it clear that the arts—things like poetry, music and drama, and writing—those things weren't luxuries, they were necessities. We needed those experiences to feed our souls and make us whole and complete individuals. "

Left: Mrs. Obama and Sindre Finnes—the husband of Norway's prime minister—tour the *Wonder* exhibit at the Renwick Gallery in Washington, DC, with the other Nordic leaders' spouses before the Nordic State Dinner. Artist Gabriel Dawe created a rainbow out of sixty miles of thread. May 13, 2016

Previous spread: Mrs. Obama welcomes girls from Morocco and Liberia in the State Dining Room before a screening of *We Will Rise: Michelle Obama's Mission to Educate Girls Around the World.* October 11, 2016

It would have been easy to make Mrs. Obama the focus of every photo. But some of the most interesting moments happen on the edges of the picture.

When Orchard Gardens students performed for Mrs. Obama and guests during a White House luncheon, they rapped about not letting circumstances define them. At one time, Orchard Gardens was one of the lowest-ranked schools in Massachusetts and in the country. In 2010, it was named a Turnaround Arts school. Three years after bringing arts into its classroom programs and giving students the opportunity to explore their creativity, Orchard Gardens had become one of the most improved schools in the state.

Mrs. Obama was so inspired by the Orchard Gardens students that she stopped by the Map Room to surprise them. The whole room burst into excitement when Mrs. Obama walked in. February 24, 2014

77

When students from the Sphinx Overture program took the stage in the East Room, it was so quiet you could hear a pin drop. The audience, which included the First Lady, waited with anticipation for the performance to begin. I held my breath and hoped these young musicians wouldn't freeze under pressure.

Then the leader of the quartet nodded and the music began. They were phenomenal! At the end of the performance, the audience erupted with joy! I could see the amazement and pride on Mrs. Obama's face.

The First Lady congratulates Sphinx Overture students following their performance during the National Arts and Humanities Youth Program Awards ceremony in the East Room.
November 15, 2016

Left: Mrs. Obama dances onstage with Matthew Morrison and Kristin Chenoweth in the East Room after a televised event, called *Broadway at the White House*. This daylong workshop featured students from public arts high schools around the country as they learned from Broadway performers and craftspeople and were treated to musical performances. November 16, 2015

Above: The cast of *Finding Neverland* gets ready for its performance in the Diplomatic Reception Room. November 16, 2015

Above: President and Mrs. Obama
attend the Kennedy Center Honors
together at the John F. Kennedy
Center for the Performing Arts in
Washington, DC. December 8, 2013

Right: A Secret Service agent opens
the door as Mrs. Obama enters the
Presidential Box for the Kennedy
Center Honors. December 6, 2015

President and Mrs. Obama usually attended the Kennedy Center Honors together, to pay tribute to the important artists being recognized that year. But on this night, Mrs. Obama came alone and took her seat in the Presidential Box while the President was delivering a heartfelt speech to the nation about a terrorist attack that occurred in San Bernardino, California.

Although it was a difficult night for our country, it was important to show the world that we were still strong. Even in our darkest times, Mrs. Obama was a shining beacon of hope, just as the arts can shine light in the darkest moments of people's lives.

CHAPTER 8

Visitor-in-Chief

My time as a White House photographer moved as quickly as our motorcade. In four years, I traveled to twenty countries and countless cities and towns across the United States. I will never forget the faces of the people we met and the places we visited. These experiences left a lasting impression.

Overseas travel was important to strengthen America's bonds with other countries. It also gave Mrs. Obama the chance to highlight issues that were important to her, especially the power of education.

> " No matter where **she** lives, every girl *deserves the chance* to live a life of her own choosing. "

Left: Mrs. Obama boards Bright Star, the official plane of the First Lady, at Orlando International Airport. July 1, 2014

Following spread: President and Mrs. Obama attend the Cannon Ball Flag Day Celebration at the Standing Rock Sioux Tribe Reservation in Cannon Ball, North Dakota. Tribal Chairman Dave Archambault II said that the First Lady's presence "shows there's a real concern for our children," because she has been such an activist for young people. June 13, 2014

Mrs. Obama traveled to China with her daughters, Sasha and Malia. The trip combined visits to schools and cultural and historic sites to promote education and encourage greater understanding between our countries.

A highlight of the trip was visiting the Great Wall of China, one of the world's greatest feats of engineering. Built in sections over the course of two thousand years, the wall stretches for thousands of miles. Its purpose was to protect China from foreign invaders.

Leaving the Great Wall was an even bigger adventure, because we found out we'd be riding a toboggan to get down from the wall.

The First Lady hugs her daughters, Sasha and Malia, atop the Great Wall of China in Mutianyu, China. March 23, 2014

I loved seeing Mrs. Obama's smiling
face as she tobogganed down the
hill with a Secret Service agent
behind her, in Mutianyu, China.
March 23, 2014

The First Lady and daughters Sasha and Malia feed apples to giant pandas during a visit to the Giant Panda Research Base in Chengdu, China. March 26, 2014

The Let Girls Learn initiative, which focuses on global education for girls, was extremely important to Mrs. Obama. I will never forget the young women we met around the world and the obstacles they had to overcome to get an education.

The First Lady is welcomed by
students at Mulberry School for Girls
in London, England. June 16, 2015

"If we get our **education**, we can do anything. We can *lift ourselves* to heights we could never *imagine*."

The First Lady meets with Prince Harry to discuss ways our countries can work together to improve education opportunities for girls around the world. June 16, 2015

Above: While in Japan to discuss the importance of the Let Girls Learn initiative, Mrs. Obama participates in a traditional tea ceremony with Caroline Kennedy, US Ambassador to Japan and daughter of former President John F. Kennedy, in Kyoto, Japan. March 20, 2015

Right: Mrs. Obama walks through a tunnel of Torii gates at Japan's Fushimi Inari Shinto Shrine. These gates mark the entrance into a sacred space. March 20, 2015

Cubans line the road to get a glimpse of the motorcade as the First Lady travels through Havana, Cuba. March 21, 2016

In 2016, President Obama became the first sitting US president to visit Cuba since Calvin Coolidge's 1928 visit. The United States blocked all interactions with Cuba when communist Fidel Castro seized control of the country in 1959. But President Obama and President Raúl Castro agreed to open communication in 2014, and more than a year later, the First Family made this historic trip.

I had always dreamed that my work would take me to faraway places. Traveling the world as part of the President and First Lady's team gave me the gift of seeing the world and all its possibilities.

Left and above: The First Family attends an exhibition baseball game between the Tampa Bay Rays and the Cuban national team at the Estadio Latinoamericano in Havana, Cuba. March 22, 2016

Mrs. Obama encouraged students to believe in themselves and not let negative voices hold them back from achieving their dreams.

" Always *stay true to* yourself and never let what somebody says distract you from *your goals*. "

Her advice made me think of my own career path and all the people who told me to get a "real" job rather than try to earn a living in the arts. Mrs. Obama's words encouraged and inspired me, just as they have for so many people around the world.

The First Lady hugs a student following a lesson about leadership and self-esteem at the Peace Corps Training Center in Kakata, Liberia. June 27, 2016

We arrived in Liberia in a rainstorm and drove for forty-five minutes on washed-out dirt roads to reach R. S. Caulfield Senior High School.

The school had no electricity and a dirt floor. But the girls were very proud of it and of the efforts they made to get to school every day. Some had to walk several hours through dangerous areas. Others had to study by candlelight after doing the cooking and cleaning for their families.

The girls were in awe that Mrs. Obama had come to see them. But Mrs. Obama was equally impressed with the students we met that day.

First Lady Michelle Obama participates in a discussion with Liberian President Ellen Johnson Sirleaf (third from left), actress Freida Pinto (left), and students at R. S. Caulfield Senior High School in Unification Town, Liberia. June 27, 2016

Leaving the White House

Mrs. Obama came from humble beginnings and has worked incredibly hard to make the world better for other people. Watching her through the lens of my camera, I learned so much about myself and the life I wanted to create.

As I walked out of the White House for the last time, I thought about all the days those gates had let me in. Just like many of those who were welcomed as guests to the Obama White House, I felt like I didn't belong there—and yet the gates still opened for me. It seemed like a dream, but I knew it was real.

What happened on the other side of those gates changed our country's history—and my life—forever.

President Barack Obama and First Lady Michelle Obama go for a hike on the Na Pohaku O Hauwahine trail in Kailua, Hawaii. January 4, 2014

Acknowledgments

I am extremely grateful for the opportunity to create this book. There are so many people who work behind the scenes to support the First Family and protect and preserve the White House: the West Wing and East Wing staff, the Executive Residence staff, the White House Medical Unit, the White House Communications Agency, the National Park Service, and the Secret Service. Thank you for so many wonderful memories. You made the long days feel much shorter by offering your support and plenty of laughs. I am thankful to call you my friends.

The White House Photo Office was filled with people who worked diligently to make sure photos were edited, printed, distributed, and archived. Janet Philips, Rick McKay, Al Anderson, Anna Ruch, Shelby Leeman, Tim Harville, Chris Mackler, Katie Waldo, Jenn Poggi, Jim Preston, Kim Hubbard, Keegan Barber, and Phaedra Singelis—I am grateful not only for your hard work and dedication but also for your constant love and encouragement. I was fortunate to work with and learn from Pete Souza, Chuck Kennedy, Lawrence Jackson, and David Lienemann. Pete Souza, thank you for being a mentor and a friend, and for giving me the opportunity of a lifetime. We will always remember the dedication, talent, and joy of our beloved photo editor, Rick McKay, whom we lost to cancer. The Photo Office became my second family and my home away from home. I am eternally grateful for all of you.

Thank you to Emily Easton for your enthusiasm, commitment, and vision. I am so grateful for the opportunity to work with you and your team at Random House Children's Books, most especially Monique Razzouk and Nicole de las Heras for the beautiful design, as well as Samantha Gentry, Allison Judd, Jenna Lisanti,

Hannah Black, Megan Williams, and Alison Kolani for your dedication to this book. A special thanks to Shelby Leeman for your talent, professionalism, and attention to detail. And thanks to Rachel Vogel for the constant support.

To Kaitlin Ketchum and the rest of the Ten Speed and Crown families—I truly appreciate your support, encouragement, and vision for *Chasing Light*.

I am nothing without my roots. To my siblings: life has been quite a journey, but we have made it together. To my father: thank you for teaching me the importance of integrity. To my mother: thank you for showing me how to be resilient. To my wonderful friends: I am so lucky for your steadiness through all of life's ups and downs. To Alan and Eden: there was always something missing until you came into my life. With your love, anything is possible.

Thank you, President Obama and Mrs. Obama, for leading our country with dignity, respect, and integrity. It has been the honor of a lifetime to serve you.